ESPECIALLY FOR:

Stanley's

FROM:

The Upson's

DATE:

_12 - 25 - 15_

A COLLECTION OF CHRISTMAS POETRY

Helen Steiner Rice

BARBOUR BOOKS
An Imprint of Barbour Publishing, Inc.

Print ISBN 978-1-62836-874-1

eBook Editions
Adobe Digital Edition (.epub) 978-1-63058-594-5
Kindle and MobiPocket Edition (.prc) 978-1-63058-595-2

Published by Barbour Books, an imprint of Barbour Publishing, Inc., P.O. Box 719, Uhrichsville, Ohio 44683, www.barbourbooks.com

Our mission is to publish and distribute inspirational products offering exceptional value and biblical encouragement to the masses.

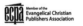
Member of the
Evangelical Christian
Publishers Association

Printed in the United States of America.

CONTENTS

INTRODUCTION

*W*e call it the most wonderful time of the year. Children make their wish lists months in advance, and by mid-November shoppers are swarming the stores. Christmas music floods the airwaves, and trees with their festive decorations go up all over town. There are programs and cantatas, parties and fun going on everywhere we look. Yes, it's all quite amazing.

Even more amazing is that all these activities and preparations culminate in one small twenty-four-hour period. Sometimes, people get what they want out of the day; and more often, they don't.

How much better would it be to share the Christmas spirit all year long? That's the question hidden in Helen Steiner Rice's beautiful poetry. Imagine what a wonderful year that would be!

LET US LIVE CHRISTMAS EVERY DAY

*C*hristmas is more than a day at the end of the year,
More than a season of joy and good cheer,
Christmas is really God's pattern for living
To be followed all year by unselfish giving. . .
For the holiday season awakens good cheer
And draws us closer to those we hold dear,
And we open our hearts and find it is good
To live among men as we always should. . .
But as soon as the tinsel is stripped from the tree
The spirit of Christmas fades silently
Into the background of daily routine
And is lost in the whirl of life's busy scene,

And all unawares we miss and forego
The greatest blessing that mankind can know. . .
For if we lived Christmas each day, as we should,
And made it our aim to always do good,
We'd find the lost key to meaningful living
That comes not from getting
      but from unselfish giving. . .
And we'd know the great joy of peace on earth
Which was the real purpose of our Savior's birth.
For in the glad tidings of the first Christmas night
God showed us the way and the truth and the light!

                                                        –HSR

Celebration

MAY CHRISTMAS COME
AGAIN AND AGAIN

Here's hoping that your Christmas
Is a time that's set apart—
A time that's filled with happiness
And sunshine in your heart. . .
And may the warmth and love you give
Return to you all year
To brighten days in many ways
And fill your life with cheer!

-HSR

BEHOLD, I BRING YOU GOOD TIDINGS
OF GREAT JOY

Glad tidings herald the Christ child's birth—
Joy to the world and peace on earth,
Glory to God. . .let all men rejoice
And hearken once more to the angel's voice.
It matters not who or what you are—
All men can behold the Christmas star,
For the star that shone is shining still
In the hearts of men of peace and goodwill.
It offers the answer to every man's need,
Regardless of color or race or creed. . .
So joining together in brotherly love,
Let us worship again our Father above,
And forgetting our own little selfish desires,
May we seek what the star of Christmas inspires.

—HSR

And suddenly there was with the angel a multitude of the heavenly host praising God, and saying, Glory to God in the highest, and on earth peace, good will toward men.

LUKE 2:13–14

Come and worship, come and worship,
Worship Christ, the newborn King.
JAMES MONTGOMERY

A CHRISTMAS PRAYER OF PRAISE

*P*raise God, the holy One,
For giving us His only Son
To live on earth as mortals do
To draw us closer, God, to You.
Praise the Father for all things
And for the message Christmas brings.
This is indeed the day of days
To raise your voice in prayers of praise—
For we would have nowhere to go
When life has ended here below,
For redemption came and salvation was won
Through Jesus Christ, the Father's Son.

–HSR

THE MYSTERY AND MIRACLE
OF HIS CREATIVE HAND

*I*n the beauty of a snowflake
  falling softly on the land
Is the mystery and miracle
  of God's great, creative hand.

-HSR

A NEW YEAR'S MEDITATION

What better time
   and what better season,
What greater occasion
   or more wonderful reason
To kneel down in prayer
   and lift our hands high
To the God of creation,
   who made earth and sky,
Who sent us His Son
   to live here among men—
And the message He brought
   is as true now as then. . .

-HSR

THE CHRISTMAS STORY

A star in the sky, an angel's voice
Telling the world—Rejoice! Rejoice!
Shepherds tending their flocks by night,
Falling in awe at this wondrous sight,
Wise men traveling across the lands
To place their gifts in the Christ child's hands,
No room at the inn, so a manger bed
Cradled in radiance the holy babe's head. . .
That is the story that's living still
In the hearts of all men.

—HSR

Joy

MAY THE STAR SHINE IN YOUR HEART

May the holy remembrance
   of that first Christmas night
Make this blessed season
   more joyous and bright. . .
And may the star of Bethlehem,
   which shone down from above,
Keep shining in your heart today
   and in the hearts of those you love.

—HSR

MORE CHRISTMAS WISHES

At Christmas may God grant you
Special gifts of joy and cheer,
And bless you for the good you do
For others through the year. . .
May you find rich satisfaction
In your daily work and prayer,
And in knowing as you serve Him
He will keep you in His care.

—HSR

Joy came down on Christmas Day

As angels came to earth

Heralding the miracle

Of our Messiah's birth.

UNKNOWN

O come, all ye faithful,

joyful and triumphant,

O come ye, O come ye, to Bethlehem.

LATIN HYMN

I AM THE LIGHT OF THE WORLD

*I*n this sick world of hatred
and violence and sin,
Where society renounces morals
and rejects discipline,
We stumble in darkness
groping vainly for light
To distinguish the difference
between wrong and right. . .
But dawn cannot follow
this night of despair
Unless faith lights a candle
in all hearts everywhere. . .
And warmed by the glow,
our hate melts away
And love lights the path
to a peaceful new day.

-HSR

HOLLY WREATHS

*W*hen holly wreaths are hanging
    upon each friendly door
And candles glow from windows
    and trees are trimmed once more,
It's pleasant to be sending
    this special wish to you
For all the season's happiness
    in everything you do.

—HSR

Whom having not seen, ye love; in whom,

though now ye see him not, yet believing,

ye rejoice with joy unspeakable and full of glory.

1 PETER 1:8

Somehow, not only for Christmas,

But all the long year through,

The joy that you give to others,

Is the joy that comes back to you.

JOHN GREENLEAF WHITTIER

A CHRISTMAS PRAYER FOR JOY

*O*ur Father, who art in heaven,
   hear this Christmas prayer,
And if it be Thy gracious will,
   may joy be everywhere—
The joy that comes from knowing
   that the holy Christ child came
To bless the earth at Christmas
   for Thy sake and in Thy name.
And with this prayer there comes a wish,
   that these holy, happy days
Will bless your loved ones everywhere
   in many joyous ways.

—HSR

Giving

THE SPIRIT OF GIVING

*E*ach year at Christmas, the spirit of giving
Adds joy to the season and gladness to living.
Knowing this happens when Christmas is here,
Why can't we continue throughout the year
To make our lives happy and abundant with living
By following each day the spirit of giving?

–HSR

GIFTS FROM GOD

*T*his brings you a million good wishes and more
For the things you cannot buy in a store—
Like faith to sustain you in times of trial,
A joy-filled heart and a happy smile,
Contentment, inner peace, and love—
All priceless gifts from God above!

-HSR

It is Christmas in the heart

that puts Christmas in the air.

W. T. ELLIS

Gifts of time and love are surely the basic

ingredients of a truly merry Christmas.

PEG BRACKEN

THE GIFT OF GOD'S LOVE

*A*ll over the world at this season,
    expectant hands reach to receive
Gifts that are lavishly fashioned—
    the finest that man can conceive. . .
For purchased and given at Christmas
    are luxuries we long to possess,
Given as favors and tokens
    to try in some way to express
That strange, indefinable feeling
    which is part of this glad time of year
When streets are crowded with shoppers
    and the air resounds with good cheer. . .

But back of each tinsel-tied package
    exchanged at this gift-giving season,
Unrecognized often by many,
    lies a deeper, more meaningful reason—
For born in a manger at Christmas
    as a gift from the Father above,
An infant whose name was called Jesus
    brought mankind the gift of God's love. . .
And the gifts that we give have no purpose
    unless God is part of the giving
And unless we make Christmas a pattern
    to be followed in everyday living.

-HSR

What can I give Him, poor as I am?

If I were a shepherd I would bring a lamb.

If I were a wise man I would do my part.

Yet what can I give Him? Give Him my heart.

CHRISTINA ROSSETTI

Every man shall give as he is able, according

to the blessing of the LORD thy God

which he hath given thee.

DEUTERONOMY 16:17

THE PRICELESS GIFT OF CHRISTMAS

*N*ow Christmas is a season
    for joy and merrymaking,
A time for gifts and presents,
    for giving and for taking,
A festive, friendly, happy time
    when everyone is gay—
But have we ever really felt
    the greatness of the day?
For through the centuries the world
    has wandered far away
From the beauty and the meaning
    of the holy Christmas Day. . .
For Christmas is a heavenly gift
    that only God can give—
It's ours just for the asking
    for as long as we shall live. . .

It can't be bought or bartered,
    it can't be won or sold,
It doesn't cost a penny,
    and it's worth far more than gold.
It isn't bright and gleaming
    for eager eyes to see—
It can't be wrapped in tinsel
    or placed beneath a tree.
It isn't soft and shimmering
    for reaching hands to touch,
Or some expensive luxury
    you've wanted very much.
For the priceless gift of Christmas
    is meant just for the heart,
And we receive it only
    when we become a part

Of the kingdom and the glory
    which is ours to freely take,
For God sent the holy Christ child
    at Christmas for our sake
So man might come to know Him
    and feel His presence near
And see the many miracles
    performed when He was here.
And this priceless gift of Christmas
    is within the reach of all—
The rich, the poor, the young and old,
    the greatest and the small.
So take His priceless gift of love—
    reach out and you receive—
And the only payment that God asks
    is just that you believe.

—HSR

Every gift which is given, even though it be small,

is in reality great, if it is given with affection.

PINDAR

Every time we love,

every time we give,

it's Christmas.

DALE EVANS ROGERS

CHRISTMAS IS A SEASON FOR GIVING

Christmas is a season
    for gifts of every kind—
All the glittery, pretty things
    that Christmas shoppers find—
Baubles, beads, and bangles
    of silver and of gold—
Anything and everything
    that can be bought or sold
Is given at this season
    to place beneath the tree,
For Christmas is a special time
    for giving lavishly.
But there's one rare and priceless gift
    that can't be sold or bought—
It's something poor or rich can give,
    for it's a loving thought. . .
And loving thoughts are blessings
    for which no one can pay,
And only loving hearts can give
    this priceless gift away.

-HSR

BEYOND OUR ASKING

*M*ore than hearts can imagine
   or minds comprehend,
God's bountiful gifts
   are ours without end.
We ask for a cupful
   when the vast sea is ours,
We pick a small rosebud
   from a garden of flowers,
We reach for a sunbeam
   but the sun still abides,
We draw one short breath
   but there's air on all sides,
Whatever we ask for
   falls short of God's giving,
For His greatness exceeds
   every facet of living.

And always God's ready
        and eager and willing
To pour out His mercy,
        completely fulfilling
All of man's needs
        for peace, joy, and rest,
For God gives His children
        whatever is best.
Just give Him a chance
        to open His treasures,
And He'll fill your life with
        unfathomable pleasures—
Pleasures that never grow
        worn out and faded
And leave us depleted,
        disillusioned and jaded—
For God has a storehouse
        just filled to the brim
With all that man needs,
        if we'll only ask Him.

—HSR

To perceive Christmas through its wrappings
becomes more difficult with every year.

E. B. WHITE

Give, and it shall be given unto you; good measure,
pressed down, and shaken together, and running over,
shall men give into your bosom. For with the same
measure that ye mete withal it shall be measured to you
again.

LUKE 6:38

THE BLESSINGS OF SHARING

*O*nly what we give away
Enriches us from day to day,
For not in getting but in giving
Is found the lasting joy of living,
For no one ever had a part
In sharing treasures of the heart
Who did not feel the impact of
The magic mystery of God's love.
And love alone can make us kind
And give us joy and peace of mind,
So live with joy unselfishly
And you'll be blessed abundantly.

−HSR

GIVING IS THE KEY TO LIVING

*C*hristmas is a season of giving
And giving is the key to living. . .
So let us give ourselves away,
Not just today but every day,
And remember, a kind and thoughtful deed
Or a hand outstretched in a time of need
Is the rarest of gifts, for it is a part
Not of the purse but a loving heart. . .
And he who gives of himself will find
True joy of heart and peace of mind.

–HSR

Maybe Christmas, the Grinch thought,

doesn't come from a store.

DR. SEUSS

Every man according as he purposeth in his heart,

so let him give; not grudgingly, or of necessity:

for God loveth a cheerful giver.

2 CORINTHIANS 9:7

HEART GIFTS

*I*t's not the things that can be bought
That are life's richest treasures,
It's just the little "heart gifts"
That money cannot measure.
A cheerful smile, a friendly word,
A sympathetic nod,
All priceless little treasures
From the storehouse of our God.
They are the things that can't be bought
With silver or with gold,
For thoughtfulness and kindness
And love are never sold.
They are the priceless things in life
For which no one can pay,
And the giver finds rich recompense
In giving them away.

-HSR

GIVE LAVISHLY! LIVE ABUNDANTLY!

The more you give, the more you get
The more you laugh, the less you fret.
The more you do unselfishly,
The more you live abundantly
The more of everything you share,
The more you'll always have to spare.
The more you love, the more you'll find
That life is good and friends are kind,
For only what we give away
Enriches us from day to day.
So let's live Christmas through the year
And fill the world with love and cheer.

–HSR

He who has not Christmas in his
heart will never find it under a tree.

Roy L. Smith

My idea of Christmas, whether old-fashioned
or modern, is very simple: loving others.
Come to think of it, why do we have to
wait for Christmas to do that?

Bob Hope

A GIFT OF JOY

As once more we approach the birthday of our King,
Do we search our hearts for a gift we can bring?
Do we stand by in awe like the small drummer boy
Who had no rare jewels, not even a toy
To lay at Christ's crib like the wise men of old,
Who brought precious gifts of silver and gold?
But the drummer boy played for the infant child,
And the baby Jesus looked up and smiled,
For the boy had given the best he had,
And his gift from the heart made the Savior glad.
Today He still smiles on all those who bring
Their hearts to lay at the feet of the King.

-HSR

Prayer

MAY CHRISTMAS RENEW
IN US A CHILDLIKE FAITH

May Christmas renew in us a childlike faith
For only then can we all endure
These changing times and feel secure,
For faith in things we cannot see
Requires a child's simplicity—
For in a small child's shining eyes
The faith of all the ages lies. . .
And tiny hands and tousled heads
That kneel in prayer by little beds
Are closer to the dear Lord's heart
And of His kingdom more a part
Than we who search and never find
The answer to our questioning minds—
For God can never be defined
By any meager, mortal mind,
And only a child can completely accept
What probing adults research and reject.
O Father, grant once more to men
A simple, childlike faith again,
For only by faith and faith alone
Can we approach our Father's throne.

—HSR

A PRAYER FOR CHRISTMAS

God, give us eyes this Christmas
   to see the Christmas star,
And give us ears to hear the song
   of angels from afar. . .
And with our eyes and ears attuned
   for a message from above,
Let Christmas angels speak to us
   of hope and faith and love—
Hope to light our pathway
   when the way ahead is dark,
Hope to sing through stormy days
   with the sweetness of a lark,
Faith to trust in things unseen
   and know beyond all seeing
That it is in our Father's love
   we live and have our being.

—HSR

God goes to those who have time to
hear Him—and so on this cloudless
night He went to simple shepherds.

MAX LUCADO

But Mary kept all these things,
and pondered them in her heart.

LUKE 2:19

GOD IS ALWAYS THERE
TO HEAR OUR PRAYER

Let us find joy in the news of His birth,
And let us find comfort and strength for each day
In knowing that Christ walked this same earthly way,
So He knows all our needs
    and He hears every prayer,
And He keeps all His children
    always safe in His care. . .
And whenever we're troubled and lost in despair,
We have but to seek Him and ask Him in prayer
To guide and direct us and help us to bear
Our sickness and sorrow, our worry and care. . .
So once more at Christmas
    let the whole world rejoice
In the knowledge He answers
    every prayer that we voice.

–HSR

LISTEN IN SILENCE IF YOU WOULD HEAR

*L*et us listen in silence so we may hear
The Christmas message more clearly this year.
Silently the green leaves grow;
In silence falls the soft, white snow. . .
Silently bright stars appear,
In silence velvet night draws near.
And silently God enters in
To free a troubled heart from sin,
For God works silently in lives,
And nothing spiritual survives
Amid the din of a noisy street
Where raucous crowds with hurrying feet
And blinded eyes and deafened ears
Are never privileged to hear
The message God wants to impart
To every troubled, weary heart.
So let not our worldly celebrations
Disturb our Christmas meditations,
For only in a quiet place
Can we behold God face-to-face.

-HSR

LEARN TO REST

*W*e all need short vacations
    in life's fast and maddening race—
An interlude of quietness
    from the constant, jet-age pace,
So when your day is pressure-packed
    and your hours are all too few
Just close your eyes and meditate
    and let God talk to you.

-HSR

A CHRISTMAS PRAYER

*O*h God, in Thy great goodness,
May our guidance Christmas night
Be the star the wise men followed—
Not a man-made satellite.

—HSR

Friends and Family

CHRISTMASTIME IS FRIENDSHIP TIME

*A*t Christmastime our hearts reach out
    to friends we think of dearly,
And checking through our friendship lists,
    as all of us do yearly,
We stop awhile to reminisce
    and to pleasantly review
Happy little happenings
    and things we used to do. . .
And though we've been too busy
    to keep in touch all year,
We send a Christmas greeting
    at this season of good cheer. . .
So Christmas is a lovely link
    between old years and new
That keeps the bond of friendship
    forever unbroken and true.

–HSR

WHY WRITE THESE CHRISTMAS GREETINGS?

I wonder if you know the real reason
I send you a card every year at this season?
Do you think it's a habit I just can't break
Or something I do just for custom's sake?
I think I should tell you it's something more
For to me Christmas opens the friendship door. . .
And I find myself reaching across the year
And clasping the hand of somebody dear.
To me it's a link I wouldn't want broken
That holds us together when words are unspoken.
For often through the year we have to forego
Exchanging good wishes with those we know,
But Christmas opens the door of the heart
And whether we're close or far apart. . .
When I write your name I think of you
And pause and reflect and always renew
The bond that exists since we first met
And I found you somebody too nice to forget.

-HSR

CHRISTMAS THANKS

*T*his comes to you with loving thoughts
When Christmastime is here—
Thoughts of all the qualities
That make you very dear. . .
And this brings you many wishes
That today and always, too,
You'll have the special happiness
That ought to come to you.

–HSR

Christmas is a season for kindling
the fire for hospitality in the hall,
the genial flame of charity in the heart.

WASHINGTON IRVING

A man that hath friends must shew himself friendly:
and there is a friend that sticketh closer than a brother.

PROVERBS 18:24

A CHRISTMAS WISH

At Christmas and always,
May you be guided by His light
And surrounded with His love.

-HSR

EVERY YEAR WHEN CHRISTMAS COMES

I have a list of folks I know
　　all written in a book
And every year when Christmas comes,
　　I go and take a look.
And that is when I realize
　　that these names are a part
Not of the book they're written in,
　　but of my very heart.
And while it sounds fantastic
　　for me to make this claim
I really feel that I'm composed
　　of each remembered name,

So never think my Christmas cards
    are just a mere routine
Of names upon a Christmas list
    forgotten in between,
For I am but the total
    of the many folks I've met,
And you happen to be one of those
    I prefer to not forget.
And every year when Christmas comes,
    I realize anew
The best gift life can offer
    is meeting folks like you—
And may the spirit of Christmas
    that forevermore endures
Leave its richest blessings
    in the hearts of you and yours.

-HSR

It's true, Christmas can feel like a lot of work, particularly for mothers. But when you look back on all the Christmases in your life, you'll find you've created family traditions and lasting memories. Those memories, good and bad, are really what help to keep a family together over the long haul.

CAROLINE KENNEDY

GREETING FRIENDS

*I*t's Christmas and time to greet you once more,
But what can I say that I've not said before
Except to repeat at this meaningful season
That I have a deeply significant reason
For sending this greeting to tell you today
How thankful I am that you passed my way.

—HSR

HUSH-A-BYE, HONEY

Hush-a-bye, hush-a-bye, my sleepy head,
Angels are waiting to tuck you in bed.
Go to sleep, go to sleep, close your bright eyes,
Nighttime is tumbling out of the skies.
Angels are waiting their vigil to keep,
The sandman is filling your wee eyes with sleep.
Hush-a-bye, baby, hush-a-bye, sweet,
Playtime is over for tired, tiny feet.
Close your eyes, honey, sleepy time's here,
Good night, little darling, good night, little dear.

-HSR

It is good to be children sometimes,

and never better than at Christmas,

when its mighty founder was a child Himself.

CHARLES DICKENS

❧

A friend loveth at all times.

PROVERBS 17:17

A NEW YEAR'S MEDITATION

At this glad season, when there's joy everywhere,
Let us meet our Redeemer at the altar of prayer,
Asking Him humbly to bless all of our days
And grant us forgiveness for our erring ways...
And though we're unworthy, dear Father above,
Accept us today and let us dwell in Thy love
So we may grow stronger upheld by Thy grace,
And with Thy assistance be ready to face
All the temptations that fill every day,
And hold on to our hands when we stumble and stray...
And thank You, dear God, for the year that now ends
And for the great blessing of loved ones and friends.

–HSR

A FAVORITE RECIPE

Take a cup of kindness, mix it well with love,
Add a lot of patience and faith in God above.
Sprinkle very generously
    with joy and thanks and cheer—
And you'll have lots of "angel food"
    to feast on all the year.

—HSR

The best of all gifts around any Christmas

tree is the presence of a happy family

all wrapped up in each other.

BURTON HILLIS

WIDEN MY VISION

God, open my eyes so I may see
And feel Your presence close to me.
Give me strength for my stumbling feet
As I battle the crowd on life's busy street,
And widen the vision of my unseeing eyes
So in passing faces I'll recognize
Not just a stranger, unloved and unknown,
But a friend with a heart that is much like my own.
Give me perception to make me aware
That scattered profusely on life's thoroughfare
Are the best gifts of God that we daily pass by
As we look at the world with an unseeing eye.

—HSR

The Meaning
of Christmas

THIS IS THE SAVIOR OF THE WORLD

All the world has heard the story
    of the little Christ child's birth,
But too few have felt the meaning
    of His mission here on earth.
Some regard the Christmas story
    as something beautiful to hear,
A lovely Christmas custom
    that we celebrate each year,
But it is more than just a story told
    to make our hearts rejoice—
It's our Father up in heaven speaking
    through the Christ child's voice,
Telling us of heavenly kingdoms
    that He has prepared above
For all who trust His mercy
    and live only for His love. . .
And only through the Christ child
    can man be born again,
for God sent the baby Jesus
    as the Savior of all men.

–HSR

THE COMFORT OF HIS LOVE

A baby was born in a manger
While a bright star shone down from above,
And the world learned the depths of God's mercy
And the comfort and strength of His love.
May the thought of that long ago Christmas
And the meaning it's sure to impart,
Bring a wonderful message of comfort
And a deep new peace to your heart.

—HSR

The hinge of history is on the
door of a Bethlehem stable.

RALPH W. SOCKMAN

And the Word was made flesh, and dwelt among us,
(and we beheld his glory, the glory as of the only
begotten of the Father,) full of grace and truth.

JOHN 1:14

THE MIRACLE OF CHRISTMAS

The wonderment in a small child's eyes,
The ageless awe in the Christmas skies,
The nameless joy that fills the air,
The throngs that kneel in praise and prayer—
These are the things that make us know
That men may come and men may go,
But none will ever find a way
To banish Christ from Christmas Day,
For with each child there's born again
A mystery that baffles men.

—HSR

ONLY WITH OUR HEARTS

With our eyes we see
The glitter of Christmas,
With our ears we hear
Its merriment,
With our hands we touch
The tinsel-tied trinkets. . .
But only with our hearts can we feel
The miracle of it.

–HSR

THE CHRISTMAS STORY

*S*ome regard the Christmas story
    as something beautiful to hear—
A dramatized tradition
    that's retold from year to year,
But it is more than just a story—
    it's God's promise to all men
That only through the Christ child
    can man be born again.
It's God's assurance of a future
    beyond all that man has dreamed. . .
For Jesus lived on earth and died
    so that man might be redeemed—

And eternal is the kingdom
  that God has prepared above
For all who trust His mercy
  and dwell daily in His love.
Mankind's hope and his salvation
  are in the Christmas story,
For in these words there are revealed
  God's greatness and His glory.

                                        –HSR

Take Christ out of Christmas,
and December becomes the bleakest
and most colorless month of the year.

A. F. WELLS

The supernatural birth of Christ,
His miracles, His resurrection and ascension,
remain eternal truths, whatever doubts may
be cast on their reality as historical facts.

DAVID FRIEDRICH STRAUSS

*O*h Father up in heaven,
    we have wandered far away
From the little holy Christ child
    that was born on Christmas Day,
And the peace on earth You promised
    we have been unmindful of,
Not believing we could find it
    in a simple thing called love.
We've forgotten why You sent us
    Jesus Christ, Your only Son,
And in arrogance and ignorance
    it's our will, not Thine, be done.
Oh, forgive us, heavenly Father,
    teach us how to be more kind
So that we may judge all people
    with our hearts and not our minds. . .
Oh, forgive us, heavenly Father,
    and help us to find the way
To understand each other
    and live Christmas every day.

–HSR

GOD IS EVERYWHERE

*O*ur Father up in heaven,
    long, long years ago,
Looked down in His great mercy
    upon the earth below
And saw that folks were lonely
    and lost in deep despair,
And so He said, "I'll send My Son
    to walk among them there
So they can hear Him speaking
    and feel His nearness, too,
And see the many miracles
    that faith alone can do. . .

For if man really sees Him
    and can touch His healing hand,
I know it will be easier
    to believe and understand."
And so the holy Christ child
    came down to live on earth,
And that is why we celebrate
    His holy, wondrous birth. . .
And that is why at Christmas
    the world becomes aware
That heaven may seem far away,
    but God is everywhere.

–HSR

Help us remember the birth of Jesus,

that we may share in the song of the angels.

ROBERT LOUIS STEVENSON

Christmas is the day that holds all time together.

ALEXANDER SMITH

WHAT IS CHRISTMAS?

Is it just a day at the end of the year—
A season of joy, merrymaking, and cheer?
Is it people and presents and glittering trees?
Oh no, it is more than any of these,
For under the tinsel and hidden from sight
Is the promise and meaning
　　of that first Christmas night
When the shepherds stood in wondered awe
And felt transformed by what they saw.
So let us not in our search for pleasure
Forego our right to this priceless treasure,
For Christmas is still a God-given day,
And let us remember to keep it that way.

-HSR

CHRISTMAS AND THE CHRIST CHILD

*I*n our Christmas celebrations
    of merriment and mirth,
Let us not forget the miracle
    of the holy Christ child's birth. . .
For in our festivities it is easy to lose sight
Of the baby in the manger
    and that holy silent night. . .
And we miss the mighty meaning
    and we lose the greater glory
Of the holy little Christ child
    and the blessedChristmas story
If we don't keep Christ in Christmas
    and make His love a part
Of all the joy and happiness
    that fill our homes and hearts.

-HSR

But while he thought on these things, behold, the angel of the LORD appeared unto him in a dream, saying, Joseph, thou son of David, fear not to take unto thee Mary thy wife: for that which is conceived in her is of the Holy Ghost. And she shall bring forth a son, and thou shalt call his name JESUS: for he shall save his people from their sins. Now all this was done, that it might be fulfilled which was spoken of the Lord by the prophet, saying, Behold, a virgin shall be with child, and shall bring forth a son, and they shall call his name Emmanuel, which being interpreted is, God with us.

MATTHEW 1:20–23

THIS IS WHAT CHRISTMAS MEANS TO ME

Christmas to me is a gift from above—
A gift of salvation born of God's love—
For far beyond what my mind comprehends,
My eternal future completely depends
On that first Christmas night centuries ago
When God sent His Son to the earth below—
For if the Christ child had not been born,
There would be no rejoicing on Easter morn.
For only because Christ was born and died
And hung on a cross to be crucified
Can worldly sinners like you and me
Be fit to live in eternity.

So Christmas is more than getting and giving—
It's the why and wherefore of infinite living.
It's the positive proof for doubting God never,
For in His kingdom, life is forever. . .
And this is the reason that on Christmas Day
I can only kneel and prayerfully say,
"Thank You, God, for sending Your Son
So that when my work on earth is done
I can look at last on Your holy face,
Knowing You saved me alone by Your grace."

-HSR

And there were in the same country shepherds
abiding in the field, keeping watch over their flock
by night. And, lo, the angel of the Lord came upon
them, and the glory of the Lord shone round about
them: and they were sore afraid. And the angel said
unto them, Fear not: for, behold, I bring you good
tidings of great joy, which shall be to all people.
For unto you is born this day in the city of David a
Saviour, which is Christ the Lord. And this shall be
a sign unto you; Ye shall find the babe wrapped in
swaddling clothes, lying in a manger.

LUKE 2:8–12

THE PRESENCE OF JESUS

*J*esus came into this world
    one glorious Christmas Eve.
He came to live right here on earth
    to help us all believe.
For God in His heaven
    knew His children all would feel
That if Jesus lived among them
    they would know that He was real
And not a far-off stranger
    who dwelt up in the sky
And knew neither joys or sorrows
    that make us laugh and cry.
And so He walked among us
    and taught us how to love
And promised us that someday
    we would dwell with Him above.
And while we cannot see Him
    as they did, face-to-face,
We know that He is everywhere,
    and not in some far-off place.

-HSR

MESSENGER OF LOVE

*L*isten—be quiet—
  perhaps you can hear
The Christmas tree speaking,
  soft and clear:
I am God's messenger of love,
  and in my Christmas dress,
I come to light your heart and home
  with joy and happiness.
I bring you pretty packages
  and longed-for gifts of love,
But most of all I bring you
  a message from above—
The message Christmas angels sang
  on that first Christmas night
When Jesus Christ, the Father's Son,
  became this dark world's light.

For though I'm tinsel-laden
    and beautiful to see,
Remember, I am much, much more
    than just a glittering tree,
More than a decoration
    to enhance the Christmas scene,
I am a living symbol
    that God's love is evergreen,
And when Christmas Day is over
    and the holidays are through,
May the joyous spirit of Christmas
    abide all year with you.
So have a merry Christmas
    in the blessed Savior's name
And thank Him for the priceless gifts
    that are ours because He came.

-HSR

And it came to pass, as the angels were gone away from

them into heaven, the shepherds said one to another,

Let us now go even unto Bethlehem, and see this thing

which is come to pass, which the Lord hath made

known unto us. And they came with haste, and found

Mary, and Joseph, and the babe lying in a manger.

And when they had seen it, they made known abroad

the saying which was told them concerning this child.

And all they that heard it wondered at those things

which were told them by the shepherds.

LUKE 2:15–18

WAS IT REALLY SO?

Was the Christ child born in a manger-bed
Without a pillow to rest His head?
Did He walk on earth and live and die
And return to God to dwell on high?
We were not there to hear or see,
But our hopes and dreams of eternity
Are centered around that holy story
When God sent us His Son in glory—
And life on earth has not been the same,
Regardless of what the skeptics claim,
For no event ever left behind
A transformation of this kind. . .
So question and search and doubt, if you will,
But the story of Christmas is living still.

—HSR

A LITTLE CHILD SHALL LEAD THEM

*G*od sent the little Christ child
So man might understand
That a little child shall lead them
To that unknown Promised Land.
For God in His great wisdom
Knew that men would rise to power
And forget His holy precepts
In their great triumphal hour. . .
He knew that they would question
And doubt the holy birth
And turn their time and talents
To the pleasures of this earth. . .

But every new discovery
Is an open avenue
To more and greater mysteries,
And man's search is never through. . .
And man can never fathom
The mysteries of the Lord
Or understand His promise
Of a heavenly reward. . .
And no one but a little child
With simple faith and love
Can lead man's straying footsteps
To higher realms above.

–HSR

As long as we know in our hearts what

Christmas ought to be, Christmas is.

ERIC SEVAREID

A CHRISTMAS MESSAGE

*L*ove is the message
   that was sent to earth
On that first holy Christmas
   that heralded Christ's birth!

-HSR

Blessings

A CHRISTMAS BLESSING

May Jesus, our Savior,
   who was born on Christmas Day,
Bless you at this season
   in a very special way.
May the beauty and the promise
   of that silent, holy night
Fill your heart with peace and happiness
   and make your new year bright.

—HSR

WISHES FOR THIS CHRISTMAS

May this Christmas season bring you
Many blessings from above,
And may the coming year be filled
With peace and joy and love.

—HSR

A CHRISTMAS PRAYER

God bless you at Christmas
And go with you through the year,
And whenever you are troubled
May you feel His presence near.
May the greatness of His mercy
And the sweetness of His peace
Bring you everlasting comfort
And the joys that never cease.

–HSR

And Mary said, My soul doth magnify the Lord,

And my spirit hath rejoiced in God my Saviour.

For he hath regarded the low estate of his handmaiden:

for, behold, from henceforth all generations shall

call me blessed. For he that is mighty hath done

to me great things; and holy is his name.

LUKE 1:46–49

WHERE THERE IS LOVE

*W*here there is love the heart is light,
Where there is love the day is bright. . .
Love changes darkness into light
And makes the heart take wingless flight.
Oh, blessed are those who walk in love,
They also walk with God above.

–HSR

DISCOVERING CHRISTMAS

*M*ay Christmas this year, amid chaos, cruelty,
   and conflict, be a blessed instrument through
   which we can find comfort, courage, and cheer in
   the communion of our hearts.
May we discover this Christmas, the sustaining
   powers of a strong faith and the abiding
   values of courage, heroism, honor,
   fellowship, and freedom.
May our material gifts be less
   and our spiritual gifts greater.
"Peace on earth, goodwill to all"
   is not an empty dream.
It is the miracle of Christmas and such miracles
   are made of faith and brave hearts.
May God bless you and may the New Year
   find us all not only safe, but free.

-HSR

THOUGHTS OF THANKS

At this time may God grant you
Special gifts of joy and cheer,
And bless you for the good you do
For others through the year. . .
May you find rich satisfaction
In your daily work and prayer,
And in knowing as you serve Him
He will keep you in His care.

—HSR

What is Christmas? It is tenderness for the past,
courage for the present, hope for the future.
It is a fervent wish that every cup may overflow
with blessings rich and eternal.

AGNES M. PAHRO

Unless we make Christmas an occasion
to share our blessings, all the snow
in Alaska won't make it "white."

BING CROSBY

SHOWERS OF BLESSINGS

*E*ach day there are showers of blessings
    sent from the Father above,
For God is a great, lavish giver,
    and there is no end to His love. . .
And His grace is more than sufficient,
    His mercy is boundless and deep,
And His infinite blessings are countless,
    and all this we're given to keep
If we but seek God and find Him
    and ask for a bounteous measure
Of this wholly immeasurable offering
    from God's inexhaustible treasure. . .
For no matter how big man's dreams are,
    God's blessings are infinitely more,
For always God's giving is greater
    than what man is asking for.

-HSR

THANK YOU, GOD, FOR EVERYTHING

Thank You, God, for everything—
    the big things and the small—
For every good gift comes from God,
    the giver of them all,
And all too often we accept
    without any thanks or praise
The gifts God sends as blessings
    each day in many ways.
And so at this time
    we offer up a prayer
To thank You, God, for giving us
    a lot more than our share.

First, thank You for the little things
     that often come our way—
The things we take for granted
     and don't mention when we pray—
The unexpected courtesy,
     the thoughtful, kindly deed,
A hand reached out to help us
     in the time of sudden need.
Oh, make us more aware, dear God,
     of little daily graces
That come to us with sweet surprise
     from never-dreamed-of places.
Then thank You for the miracles
     we are much too blind to see,
and give us new awareness
     of our many gifts from Thee.
And help us to remember
     that the key to life and living
Is to make each prayer a prayer of thanks
     and each day a day of thanksgiving.

-HSR

Peace

A BEAUTIFUL BEGINNING
FOR PEACE ON EARTH

*L*et us all remember
    when our faith is running low,
Christ is more than just a figure
    wrapped in an ethereal glow. . .
For He came and dwelled among us
    and He knows our every need,
And He loves and understands us
    and forgives each sinful deed.
He was crucified and buried
    and rose again in glory,
And His promise of salvation
    makes the wondrous Christmas story
An abiding reassurance that
    the little Christ child's birth
Was the beautiful beginning
    of God's plan for peace on earth.

-HSR

A CHRISTMAS PRAYER FOR PEACE

*W*e pray to Thee, our Father,
    as Christmas comes again,
For peace among all nations
    and goodwill between all men.
Give us the strength and courage
    to search ourselves inside
And recognize our vanity,
    our selfishness, and pride. . .
For the struggle of all ages
    is centered deep within,
Where each man has his private war
    that his own soul must win. . .
For a world of peace and plenty,
    of which all men have dreamed,
Can only be attained and kept
    when the spirit is redeemed.

–HSR

And let the peace of God rule in your hearts.

Colossians 3:15

Now the God of hope fill you with all joy and

peace in believing, that ye may abound in hope,

through the power of the Holy Ghost.

Romans 15:13

A CHRISTMAS PRAYER

O God, our help in ages past,
    our hope in years to be,
Look down upon this present
    and see our need of Thee. . .
For in this age of unrest,
    with danger all around,
We need Thy hand to lead us
    to a higher, safer ground.
We need Thy help and counsel
    to make us more aware
That our safety and security
    lie solely in Thy care,
And so we pray this Christmas
    to feel Thy presence near
And for Thy all-wise guidance
    throughout the coming year.

First, give us understanding,
    enough to make us kind,
So we may judge all people
    with our hearts and not our minds.
Then give us strength and courage
    to be honorable and true,
And place our trust implicitly
    in unseen things and You...
And help us when we falter
    and renew our faith each day
And forgive our human errors
    and hear us when we pray,
And keep us gently humble
    in the greatness of Thy love
So someday we are fit to dwell
    with Thee in peace above.

–HSR

Peace came down on Christmas Day to
fill the hearts of men with all the sweet
tranquility each Christmas brings again.

UNKNOWN

Blessed are the peacemakers: for they
shall be called the children of God.

MATTHEW 5:9

MAY GOD DWELL IN US AGAIN

There is no thinking person
    who can stand untouched today
And view the world around us
    slowly drifting to decay
Without feeling deep within him
    a silent, unnamed dread
As he contemplates the future
    that lies frighteningly ahead. . .
For like watching storm clouds gather
    in a dark and threatening sky,
Man knows that there is nothing
    he can formulate or try
That will stop the storm from breaking
    in its fury and its force. . .

So as the clouds of chaos gather
    in man's muddled mind
And he searches for the answer
    he alone can never find,
Let us recognize we're facing problems
    man has never solved,
And with all our daily efforts
    life grows more and more involved. . .
But our future will seem brighter
    and we'll meet with less resistance
If we call upon our Father
    and seek divine assistance,

For the spirit can unravel
     many tangled, knotted threads
That defy the skill and power
     of the world's best hands and heads,
And our plans for growth and progress,
     of which we all have dreamed,
Cannot survive materially
     unless our spirits are redeemed. . .
So may our prayer this Christmas be
     that God may dwell again
In human hearts throughout the world
     and bring goodwill to men.

-HSR

Hark! the herald angels sing,

"Glory to the newborn King;

Peace on earth, and mercy mild,

God and sinners reconciled!"

Charles Wesley

GLORY TO GOD

*G*lory to God in the highest
 and peace on earth to men"—
May the Christmas song the angels sang
 stir in our hearts again
And bring a new awareness
 that the fate of every nation
Is sealed securely in the hand
 of the Maker of creation.
For man, with all his knowledge,
 his inventions, and his skill,
Can never go an inch beyond
 the holy Father's will,
And when we fully recognize
 the helplessness of man
And seek our Father's guidance
 in our every thought and plan,
Then only can we build a world
 of faith and hope and love,
And only then can man achieve
 the life he's dreaming of.

—HSR

A SEASON OF KINDNESS

May the kindly spirit of Christmas
    spread its radiance far and wide,
So all the world may feel the glow
    of this holy Christmastide.
Then may every heart and home
    continue through the year
To feel the warmth and wonder
    of this season of good cheer.
And may it bring us closer
    to God and to each other
Till every stranger is a friend
    and every man a brother.

-HSR

I truly believe that if we keep telling the Christmas story, singing the Christmas songs, and living the Christmas spirit, we can bring joy and happiness and peace to this world.

NORMAN VINCENT PEALE

Behold, how good and how pleasant it is for brethren to dwell together in unity!

PSALM 133:1

THE MIRACLE OF CHRISTMAS

*M*iracles are marvels
That defy all explanation
And Christmas is a miracle
And not just a celebration—
For when the true significance
Of this so-called Christmas story
Penetrates the minds of men
And transforms them with its glory,
Then only can rebellious man,
So hate-torn with dissension,
Behold his adversaries
With a broader new dimension—

For we can only live in peace
When we learn to love each other
And accept all human beings
With the compassion of a brother—
And it takes the Christ of Christmas
To change man's point of view,
For only through the Christ child
Can all men be born anew. . .
And in the Christmas story
Of the holy Christ child's birth
Is the answer to a better world
And goodwill and peace on earth.

-HSR

For unto us a child is born, unto us a son is given:

and the government shall be upon his shoulder: and

his name shall be called Wonderful, Counsellor, The

mighty God, The everlasting Father,

The Prince of Peace.

ISAIAH 9:6

Peace I leave with you, my peace I give unto you:

not as the world giveth, give I unto you.

Let not your heart be troubled.

JOHN 14:27

THE FORTRESS OF PEACE WITHIN

Peace is not something you fight for
  with bombs and missiles that kill—
Peace is attained in the silence
  that comes when the heart stands still. . .
For hearts that are restless and warlike
  with longings that never cease
Can never contribute ideas
  that bring the world nearer to peace. . .
For as dew never falls on a morning
  that follows a dark, stormy night,
The peace and grace of our Father
  fall not on a soul in flight. . .
So if we seek peace for all people,
  there is but one place to begin,
And the armament race will not win it,
  for the fortress of peace is within.

-HSR

THE FIRST CHRISTMAS MORN

*I*n this world of violence and hatred and greed
Where men lust for power and scorn those in need,
What could we hope for and where could we go
To find comfort and courage on this earth below
If in Bethlehem's manger Christ had not been born
Many centuries ago on the first Christmas morn?
For life everlasting and eternal glory
Were promised to man in the Christmas story.

–HSR

Glory be to God on high,

And peace on earth descend.

CHARLES WESLEY

"What means that star?" the shepherds said. . .

And angels, answering overhead, sang,

"Peace on earth, goodwill to men!"

JAMES RUSSELL LOWELL

MAY YOU FEEL THE QUIET BEAUTY

May you feel the quiet beauty
of that holy, silent night
When God sent the little Christ child
to be this dark world's light.
May you know the peace He promised,
may you feel His presence near,
Not only just at Christmas,
but throughout a happy year.

-HSR

THE PRAYER OF PEACE

*O*ur Father up in heaven,
    hear this fervent prayer—
May the people of all nations
    be united in Thy care. . .
For earth's peace and man's salvation
    can come only by Thy grace.

–HSR

WITH HIS LOVE

If you found any beauty in the poems in this book
    or some peace and comfort in a word or a line,
Don't give me the praise or the worldly acclaim,
    for the words that you read are not mine.
I borrowed them all to share with you
    from our heavenly Father above,
And the joy that you felt was God speaking to you
    as He flooded your heart with His love.

-HSR

Index

Helen Steiner Rice (1900–1981) has been called the "poet laureate of inspirational verse." The Ohio native worked as a greeting card editor before she began writing poems.

Also from Barbour Publishing

Here's your invitation to deeper intimacy with your loving heavenly Father—with this devotional classic from Frances J. Roberts. This powerful book, featuring lightly-updated text and scripture from the New King James Version of the Bible, shares the ministering spirit of the heavenly Father when you need a little encouragement, hope, comfort, and conviction. Through compelling prose and poetry, author Frances J. Roberts will challenge you to a deeper intimacy with God.

ISBN 978-1-62836-660-0

Available wherever Christian books are sold.